A LOOK AT SPACE SCIENCE

GALAXIES

I0817362

BY BERT WILBERFORCE

Gareth Stevens PUBLISHING

Please visit our website, www.garethstevens.com. For a free color catalog of all our high-quality books, call toll free 1-800-542-2595 or fax 1-877-542-2596.

Library of Congress Cataloging-in-Publication Data
Names: Wilberforce, Bert, author.
Title: Galaxies / Bert Wilberforce.
Description: New York : Gareth Stevens Publishing, [2021] | Series: A look at space science | Includes bibliographical references and index. | Contents: Our great galaxy! -- What is a galaxy? -- The Milky Way -- Galaxy shapes -- At the center -- How many galaxies? -- Neighboring galaxies -- How galaxies form -- Solving space mysteries -- Classes of galaxies
Identifiers: LCCN 2019045238 | ISBN 9781538259368 (library binding) | ISBN 9781538259344 (paperback) | ISBN 9781538259351 (6 Pack) | ISBN 9781538259375 (ebook)
Subjects: LCSH: Galaxies--Juvenile literature.
Classification: LCC QB857.3 .W55 2021 | DDC 523.1/12--dc23
LC record available at https://lccn.loc.gov/2019045238

First Edition

Published in 2021 by
Gareth Stevens Publishing
111 East 14th Street, Suite 349
New York, NY 10003

Copyright © 2021 Gareth Stevens Publishing

Designer: Sarah Liddell
Editor: Therese Shea

Photo credits: Cover, p. 1 (main) Triff/Shutterstock.com; background used throughout Zakharchuk/Shutterstock.com; p. 5 NASA images/Shutterstock.com; p. 7 Frokor/Wikimedia Commons; p. 9 structuresxx/Shutterstock.com; p. 11 sripfoto/Shutterstock.com; pp. 13 (both), 15 (irregular galaxy), 30 (lenticular galaxy) Tryphon/Wikimedia Commons; pp. 15 (elliptical galaxy), 30 (elliptical galaxy) Huntster/Wikimedia Commons; p. 15 (lenticular galaxy) QAI Publishing/Contributor/Universal Images Group/Getty Images; pp. 17, 19, 29 Vadim Sadovski/Shutterstock.com; p. 21 Mylkomeda/Wikimedia Commons; p. 23 WilliamKF/Wikimedia Commons; p. 25 Pine/Wikimedia Commons; p. 27 Zeimusu/Wikimedia Commons; p. 30 (spiral galaxy) Rotatebot/Wikimedia Commons; p. 30 (irregular galaxy) BesigedB~commonswiki/Wikimedia Commons.

All rights reserved. No part of this book may be reproduced in any form without permission in writing from the publisher, except by a reviewer.

Printed in the United States of America

Some of the images in this book illustrate individuals who are models. The depictions do not imply actual situations or events.

CPSIA compliance information: Batch #CS20GS: For further information contact Gareth Stevens, New York, New York at 1-800-542-2595.

Find us on

CONTENTS

Words in the glossary appear in **bold** type the first time they are used in the text.

OUR GREAT GALAXY!

The *Star Wars* movies start with the line: "A long time ago in a galaxy far, far away . . ." What is a galaxy? Where are we in our galaxy? How did our galaxy form? Read on to **explore** our galaxy and others!

MAKE THE GRADE

Scientists didn't know galaxies other than our own existed until the early 1900s.

WHAT IS A GALAXY?

A galaxy is a group of stars, **planets**, gas, dust, and other objects that travel through space together. Our sun is a star. All the objects in our solar system, including Earth, are a part of the Milky Way galaxy.

MAKE THE GRADE

A solar system is made up of a star and everything that orbits, or moves around, it.

THE MAGNIFICENT MILKY WAY

The Milky Way galaxy is named for a band of gas clouds and stars in the night sky. It looks milky, or whitish. In fact, nearly every star that you can see without a **telescope** is part of the Milky Way galaxy.

MAKE THE GRADE

This picture shows the "milky" band that gives our galaxy its name.

If almost every star you can see is a part of our galaxy, you can tell that it's hard to say how many stars are in it! Scientists estimate, or guess, that there are about 100 **billion** stars in the Milky Way!

MAKE THE GRADE

Our solar system travels around the Milky Way's center. It takes more than 200 **million** years to finish one orbit!

GALAXY SHAPES

Scientists group galaxies by their shape. **Spiral** galaxies look like they have "arms" of gas, dust, and stars that spiral out of the center. The Milky Way is a barred spiral galaxy because the middle looks like it was **stretched** into a bar shape.

MAKE THE GRADE

The Hubble Space Telescope has helped scientists put together pictures of galaxies like these.

Elliptical galaxies are shaped like ellipticals, or flat circles. They don't look like a disk as spiral galaxies do. **Lenticular** galaxies are even flatter. Irregular galaxies don't seem to have any sort of regular, or common, shape at all.

MAKE THE GRADE

Collisions between galaxies can affect their shapes!

LENTICULAR GALAXY

ELLIPTICAL GALAXY

IRREGULAR GALAXY

AT THE CENTER

At the center of our galaxy is a large black hole. This is a place with a very powerful force of **gravity**. Anything that gets close gets sucked in—even light. Black holes can't be seen, but their pull on objects around them can.

MAKE THE GRADE

Our sun is about 27,000 **light-years** from the center of the galaxy.

HOW MANY GALAXIES?

Just as it's hard to know how many stars are in our own galaxy, it's hard to know how many galaxies are in the **universe**. Some scientists think there could be around 100 billion galaxies in all!

HUBBLE SPACE TELESCOPE

MAKE THE GRADE

The Hubble Space Telescope watched one small spot in space for 12 days—and counted 10,000 galaxies!

NEIGHBORING GALAXIES

The closest galaxy to the Milky Way is called the Canis Major Dwarf Galaxy. It's 25,000 light-years from the sun. So, a person traveling from the sun to this galaxy at the speed of light would seem to take 25,000 Earth years to get there!

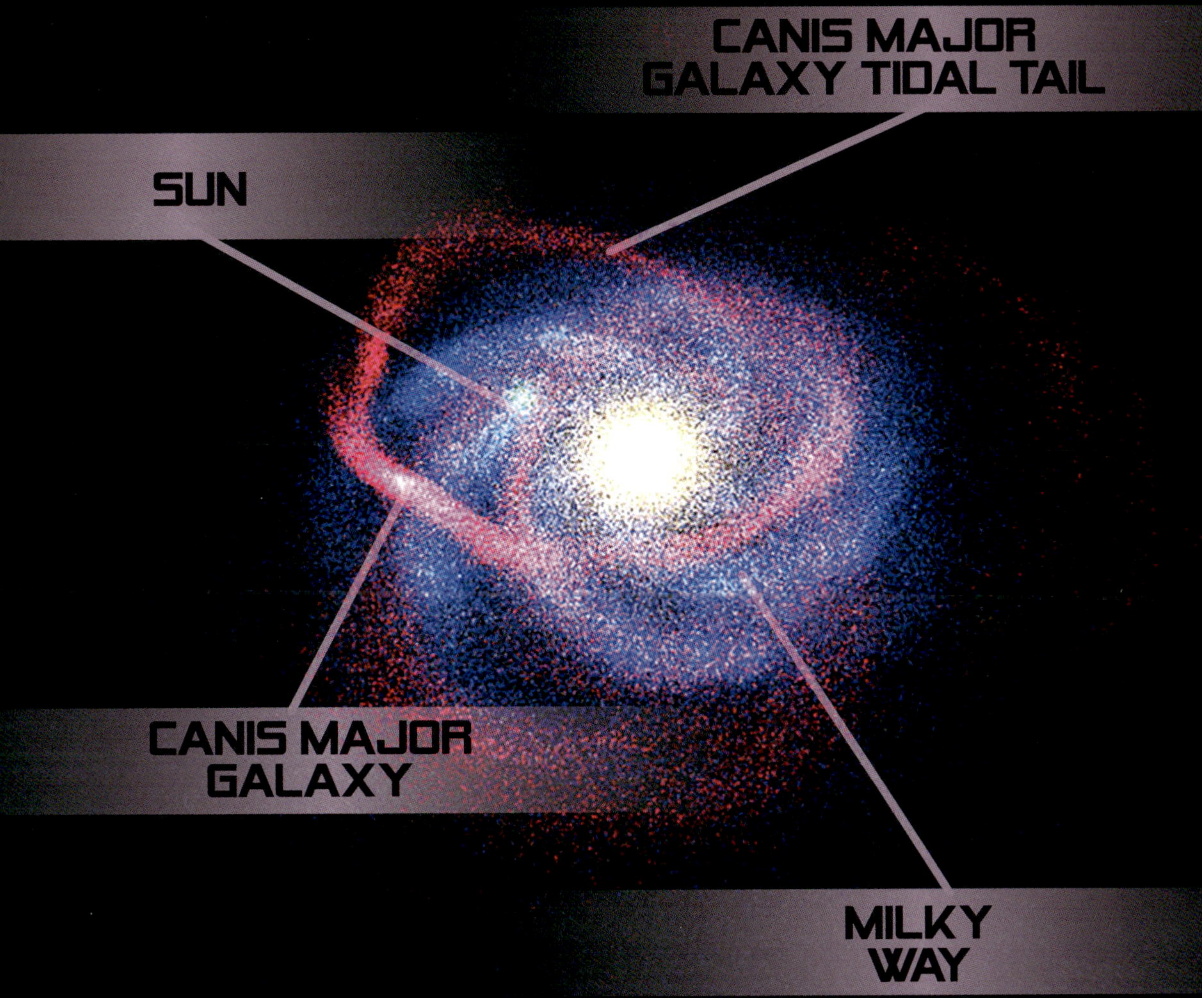

MAKE THE GRADE

The Canis Major Dwarf Galaxy has tidal tails, or streams of gas and stars, that wrap around the Milky Way!

Other close galaxies are the Large Magellanic Cloud and the Small Magellanic Cloud. Early **astronomers** spotted these galaxies long ago. The explorer Ferdinand Magellan wrote about them during his travels around the world in 1519. They're named for him.

MAKE THE GRADE

This cluster, or group of stars, was thought to be in the Milky Way. Now scientists think it's in the Sagittarius Dwarf Elliptical Galaxy, another nearby galaxy.

HOW GALAXIES FORM

NASA scientists think galaxies begin as clouds of dust and stars. The force of gravity causes these objects to draw together and sometimes collide. Stars and other space objects form and begin their orbits around the center of the galaxy.

MAKE THE GRADE

It took billions of years for large galaxies to form.

Even today, galaxies are re-forming as they collide with other galaxies. They make even larger galaxies. The Andromeda galaxy is headed toward the Milky Way. The galaxies will likely collide, but not until billions of years from now.

TWO GALAXIES MERGING

MAKE THE GRADE

Scientists think most large galaxies are the result of the merging, or joining, of smaller galaxies.

SOLVING SPACE MYSTERIES

NASA's James Webb Space Telescope will study the first galaxies and help us understand more about how they formed and grew. This will lead to discoveries about our universe. There are still many mysteries to figure out about our galaxy and beyond!

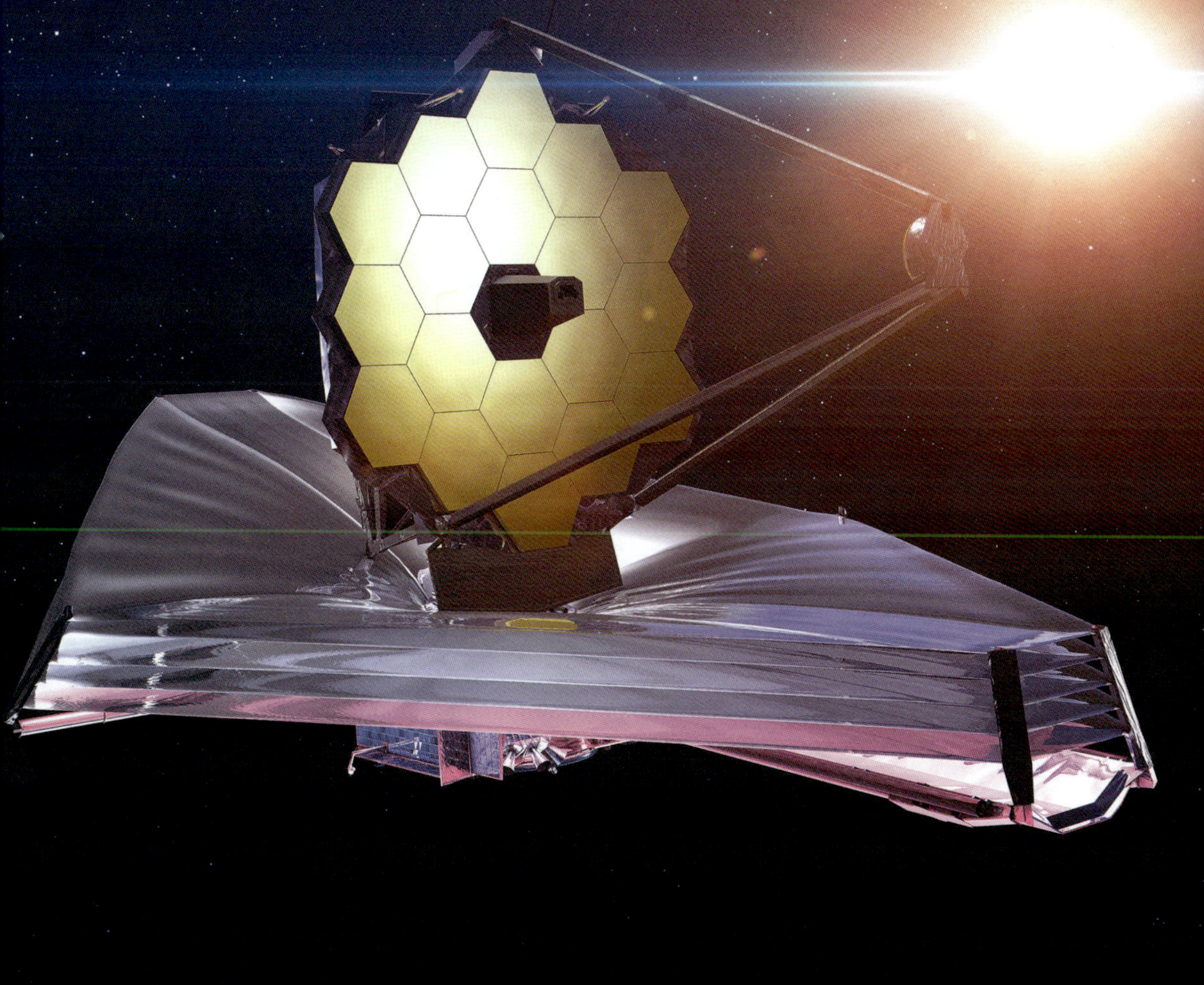
JAMES WEBB SPACE TELESCOPE

MAKE THE GRADE

The Milky Way Galaxy is more than 13 billion years old. Scientists know this by figuring out the age of its oldest stars.

CLASSES OF GALAXIES

SPIRAL

ELLIPTICAL

IRREGULAR

LENTICULAR

GLOSSARY

astronomer: a person who studies stars, planets, and other heavenly bodies

billion: 1,000 million, or 1,000,000,000

collision: the act of two objects hitting each other

explore: to search in order to find out new things

gravity: the force that pulls objects toward the center of a planet, star, or black hole

lenticular: of or relating to a lens or the shape of a lens

light-year: the distance light can travel in 1 year

million: a thousand thousands, or 1,000,000

planet: a large round object that moves around a star

spiral: a shape or line that curls outward from a center point. Also, to move outward in a curling shape.

stretched: describing something that looks wider after being pulled

telescope: a tool that makes faraway objects look bigger and closer

universe: everything that exists in space

FOR MORE INFORMATION

BOOKS

Hudak, Heather C. *Galaxies*. Minneapolis, MN: Checkerboard Library, 2017.

Rathburn, Betsy. *Galaxies*. Minneapolis, MN: Bellwether Media, Inc., 2019.

WEBSITES

Galaxy Facts for Kids
www.sciencekids.co.nz/sciencefacts/space/galaxies.html
Find many cool galaxy facts here.

What Is a Galaxy?
spaceplace.nasa.gov/galaxy/en/
Read more on this NASA site, and make a galaxy model!

Publisher's note to educators and parents: Our editors have carefully reviewed this website to ensure that it is suitable for students. Many websites change frequently, however, and we cannot guarantee that a site's future contents will continue to meet our high standards of quality and educational value. Be advised that students should be closely supervised whenever they access the internet.

INDEX